The Mind-Reader

Also by Richard Wilbur

The Beautiful Changes and Other Poems

Ceremony and Other Poems

A Bestiary
(editor, with Alexander Calder)

Molière's *The Misanthrope*
(translator)

Things of This World
(poems)

Poems 1943–1956

Candide
(comic opera, with Lillian Hellman)

Poe: Complete Poems
(editor)

Advice to a Prophet and Other Poems

Molière's *Tartuffe*
(translator)

The Poems of Richard Wilbur

Loudmouse
(for children)

Shakespeare: Poems
(co-editor, with Alfred Harbage)

Walking to Sleep: New Poems and Translations

Molière's *The School for Wives*
(translator)

Opposites
(for children and others)

The Mind-Reader

New Poems by Richard Wilbur

Harcourt Brace Jovanovich
New York and London

"To the Etruscan Poets" is copyright © 1975 by *The Ontario Review,* where
it first appeared. "A Storm in April," "The Eye," "In Limbo," "A Sketch,"
"The Fourth of July," "To His Skeleton," "John Chapman," "Children of
Darkness," and "Rillons, Rillettes" appeared originally in *The New Yorker.*
The translation from Jean de La Fontaine was first published in *A Bestiary*
(Pantheon Books). Other poems and translations first appeared in *The
American Poetry Review, The American Scholar, The Antioch Review,
The Atlantic Monthly, The Boston University Journal, The Georgia Review,
The Hollins Critic, Michigian Quarterly Review, Mill Mountain Review, The
New Republic, New York Review of Books, The Paris Review, Ploughshares,
Strike News, Tri-Quarterly,* and *The Vassar Review.* The translation
from Joseph Brodsky was issued as a broadside by Ardis Publishers, and a
broadside of "Two Riddles from Aldhelm" was published by Rook Press. The
translations of poems by Andrei Voznesensky are to be included in *Walking
on the Water,* by Andrei Voznesensky, to be published by Doubleday &
Company, Inc., and are used with their permission.

Library of Congress Cataloging in Publication Data

Wilbur, Richard, 1921–
The mind-reader.

I. Title.
PS3545.I32165M5   811'.5'2   75-42312
ISBN 0-15-160110-0

A B C D E F G H I J

For Charlee

Jusqu' à la fin du monde, lon-la

Contents

Part One

The Eye

A Storm in April

for Ben

Some winters, taking leave,
Deal us a last, hard blow,
Salting the ground like Carthage
Before they will go.

But the bright, milling snow
Which throngs the air today—
It is a way of leaving
So as to stay.

The light flakes do not weigh
The willows down, but sift
Through the white catkins, loose
As petal-drift,

Or in an up-draft lift
And glitter at a height,
Dazzling as summer's leaf-stir
Chinked with light.

This storm, if I am right,
Will not be wholly over
Till green fields, here and there,
Turn white with clover,

And through chill air the puffs of milkweed hover.

The Writer

In her room at the prow of the house
Where light breaks, and the windows are tossed with linden,
My daughter is writing a story.

I pause in the stairwell, hearing
From her shut door a commotion of typewriter-keys
Like a chain hauled over a gunwale.

Young as she is, the stuff
Of her life is a great cargo, and some of it heavy:
I wish her a lucky passage.

But now it is she who pauses,
As if to reject my thought and its easy figure.
A stillness greatens, in which

The whole house seems to be thinking,
And then she is at it again with a bunched clamor
Of strokes, and again is silent.

I remember the dazed starling
Which was trapped in that very room, two years ago;
How we stole in, lifted a sash

And retreated, not to affright it;
And how for a helpless hour, through the crack of the door,
We watched the sleek, wild, dark

And iridescent creature
Batter against the brilliance, drop like a glove
To the hard floor, or the desk-top,

And wait then, humped and bloody,
For the wits to try it again; and how our spirits
Rose when, suddenly sure,

It lifted off from a chair-back,
Beating a smooth course for the right window
And clearing the sill of the world.

It is always a matter, my darling,
Of life or death, as I had forgotten. I wish
What I wished you before, but harder.

To the Etruscan Poets

Dream fluently, still brothers, who when young
Took with your mothers' milk the mother tongue,

In which pure matrix, joining world and mind,
You strove to leave some line of verse behind

Like a fresh track across a field of snow,
Not reckoning that all could melt and go.

The Eye

". . . all this beastly seeing"
—D. H. Lawrence

for John and Bill

I.   One morning in St. Thomas, when I tried
Our host's binoculars, what was magnified?
In the green slopes about us, only green,
Brisked into fronds and paddles, could be seen,
Till by a lunging focus I was shown
Some portion of a terrace like our own.
Someone with ankles crossed, in tennis shoes,
Was turning sun-blank pages of the news,
To whom in time came espadrilles of pink
Bearing a tall and fruit-crowned tropic drink.
How long I witnessed, missing not a sip!—
Then, scanning down through photons to a ship
In the blue bay, spelt out along the bow
The queenly legend of her name; and now
Followed her shuttling lighter as it bore
Her jounced, gay charges landward to explore
Charlotte Amalie, with its duty-free
Leicas, binoculars, and jewelry.
What kept me goggling all that hour? The nice
Discernment of a lime or lemon slice?
A hope of lewd espials? An astounded
Sense of the import of a thing surrounded—
Of what a Z or almond-leaf became
Within the sudden premise of a frame?
All these, and that my eye should flutter there,
By shrewd promotion, in the outstretched air,
An unseen genius of the middle distance,
Giddy with godhead or with nonexistence.

7

II.   Preserve us, Lucy,
From the eye's nonsense, you by whom
Benighted Dante was beheld,
To whom he was beholden.

If the salesman's head
Rolls on the seat-back of the 'bus
In ugly sleep, his open mouth
Banjo-strung with spittle,

Forbid my vision
To take itself for a curious angel.
Remind me that I am here in body,
A passenger, and rumpled.

Charge me to see
In all bodies the beat of spirit,
Not merely in the *tout en l'air*
Or double pike with layout

But in the strong,
Shouldering gait of the legless man,
The calm walk of the blind young woman
Whose cane touches the curbstone.

Correct my view
That the far mountain is much diminished,
That the fovea is prime composer,
That the lid's closure frees me.

Let me be touched
By the alien hands of love forever,
That this eye not be folly's loophole
But giver of due regard.

Sleepless at Crown Point

All night, this headland
Lunges into the rumpling
Capework of the wind.

Piccola Commedia

He is no one I really know,
The sun-charred, gaunt young man
By the highway's edge in Kansas
Thirty-odd years ago.

On a tourist-cabin veranda
Two middle-aged women sat;
One, in a white dress, fat,
With a rattling glass in her hand,

Called "Son, don't you feel the heat?
Get up here into the shade."
Like a good boy, I obeyed,
And was given a crate for a seat

And an Orange Crush and gin.
"This state," she said, "is hell."
Her thin friend cackled, "Well, dear,
You've gotta fight sin with sin."

"No harm in a drink; my stars!"
Said the fat one, jerking her head.
"And I'll take no lip from Ed,
Him with his damn cigars."

Laughter. A combine whined
On past, and dry grass bent
In the backwash; liquor went
Like an ice-pick into my mind.

Beneath her skirt I spied
Two sea-cows on a floe.
"Go talk to Mary Jo, son,
She's reading a book inside."

As I gangled in at the door
A pink girl, curled in a chair,
Looked up with an ingénue stare.
Screenland lay on the floor.

Amazed by her starlet's pout
And the way her eyebrows arched,
I felt both drowned and parched.
Desire leapt up like a trout.

"Hello," she said, and her gum
Gave a calculating crack.
At once, from the lightless back
Of the room there came the grumble

Of someone heaving from bed,
A Zippo's click and flare,
Then, more and more apparent,
The shuffling form of Ed,

Who neither looked nor spoke
But moved in profile by,
Blinking one gelid eye
In his elected smoke.

This is something I've never told,
And some of it I forget.
But the heat! I can feel it yet,
And that conniving cold.

A Wedding Toast

M. C. H.
C. H. W.
14 July 1971

St. John tells how, at Cana's wedding-feast,
The water-pots poured wine in such amount
That by his sober count
There were a hundred gallons at the least.

It made no earthly sense, unless to show
How whatsoever love elects to bless
Brims to a sweet excess
That can without depletion overflow.

Which is to say that what love sees is true;
That the world's fullness is not made but found.
Life hungers to abound
And pour its plenty out for such as you.

Now, if your loves will lend an ear to mine,
I toast you both, good son and dear new daughter.
May you not lack for water,
And may that water smack of Cana's wine.

March

Beech leaves which might have clung
Parching for six weeks more
Were stripped by last night's gale
Which made so black a roar

And drove the snow-streaks level.
So we see in the glare
Of a sun whose white combustion
Cannot warm the air.

From the edge of the woods, in gusts,
The leaves are scuttled forth
Onto a pasture drifted
Like tundras of the north,

To migrate there in dry
Skitter or fluttered brawl,
Then flock into some hollow
Like this, below the wall,

With veins swept back like feathers
To our prophetic sight,
And bodies of gold shadow
Pecking at sparks of light.

In Limbo

What rattles in the dark? The blinds at Brewster?
I am a boy then, sleeping by the sea,
Unless that clank and chittering proceed
From a bent fan-blade somewhere in the room,
The air-conditioner of some hotel
To which I came too dead-beat to remember.
Let me, in any case, forget and sleep.
But listen: under my billet window, grinding
Through the shocked night of France, I surely hear
A convoy moving up, whose treads and wheels
Trouble the planking of a wooden bridge.

For a half-kindled mind that flares and sinks,
Damped by a slumber which may be a child's,
How to know when one is, or where? Just now
The hinged roof of the Cinema Vascello
Smokily opens, beaming to the stars
Crashed majors of a final panorama,
Or else that spume of music, wafted back
Like a girl's scarf or laughter, reaches me
In adolescence and the Jersey night,
Where a late car, tuned in to wild casinos,
Guns past the quiet house towards my desire.

Now I could dream that all my selves and ages,
Pretenders to the shadowed face I wear,
Might, in this clearing of the wits, forgetting
Deaths and successions, parley and atone.
It is my voice which prays it; mine replies
With stammered passion or the speaker's pause,
Rough banter, slogans, timid questionings—
Oh, all my broken dialects together;
And that slow tongue which mumbles to invent

The language of the mended soul is breathless,
Hearing an infant howl demand the world.

Someone is breathing. Is it I? Or is it
Darkness conspiring in the nursery corner?
Is there another lying here beside me?
Have I a cherished wife of thirty years?
Far overhead, a long susurrus, twisting
Clockwise or counterclockwise, plunges east,
Twin floods of air in which our flagellate cries,
Rising from love-bed, childbed, bed of death,
Swim toward recurrent day. And farther still,
Couched in the void, I hear what I have heard of,
The god who dreams us, breathing out and in.

Out of all that I fumble for the lamp-chain.
A room condenses and at once is true—
Curtains, a clock, a mirror which will frame
This blinking mask the light has clapped upon me.
How quickly, when we choose to live again,
As Er once told, the cloudier knowledge passes!
I am a truant portion of the all
Misshaped by time, incorrigible desire
And dear attachment to a sleeping hand,
Who lie here on a certain day and listen
To the first birdsong, homelessly at home.

A Sketch

Into the lower right
Square of the window frame
There came
        with scalloped flight

A goldfinch, lit upon
The dead branch of a pine,
Shining,
        and then was gone,

Tossed in a double arc
Upward into the thatched
And cross-hatched
        pine-needle dark.

Briefly, as fresh drafts stirred
The tree, he dulled and gleamed
And seemed
        more coal than bird,

Then, dodging down, returned
In a new light, his perch
A birch-
        twig, where he burned

In the sun's broadside ray,
Some seed pinched in his bill.
Yet still
        he did not stay,

But into a leaf-choked pane,
Changeful as even in heaven,
Even
        in Saturn's reign,

Tunneled away and hid.
And then? But I cannot well
Tell you
          all that he did.

It was like glancing at rough
Sketches tacked on a wall,
And all
          so less than enough

Of gold on beaten wing,
I could not choose that one
Be done
          as the finished thing.

Peter

There at the story's close
We could not stay awake.
The new wine made us doze,
And not for Jesus' sake

I struck the high-priest's slave
Who came at start of day,
But as a hand might wave
Some bugling fly away.

That hand warm by the flame,
I murmured no, no, no
To mutters of his name
And felt the rooster's crow

Flail me, yet did not waken
Out of that rocky sleep.
Dungeoned I stood there, shaken
Only enough to weep,

Only enough to fill,
At those predicted jeers,
Through the dropped lashes' grille
The socket's moat of tears.

Cottage Street, 1953

Framed in her phoenix fire-screen, Edna Ward
Bends to the tray of Canton, pouring tea
For frightened Mrs. Plath; then, turning toward
The pale, slumped daughter, and my wife, and me,

Asks if we would prefer it weak or strong.
Will we have milk or lemon, she enquires?
The visit seems already strained and long.
Each in his turn, we tell her our desires.

It is my office to exemplify
The published poet in his happiness,
Thus cheering Sylvia, who has wished to die;
But half-ashamed, and impotent to bless,

I am a stupid life-guard who has found,
Swept to his shallows by the tide, a girl
Who, far from shore, has been immensely drowned,
And stares through water now with eyes of pearl.

How large is her refusal; and how slight
The genteel chat whereby we recommend
Life, of a summer afternoon, despite
The brewing dusk which hints that it may end.

And Edna Ward shall die in fifteen years,
After her eight-and-eighty summers of
Such grace and courage as permit no tears,
The thin hand reaching out, the last word *love,*

Outliving Sylvia who, condemned to live,
Shall study for a decade, as she must,
To state at last her brilliant negative
In poems free and helpless and unjust.

The Fourth of July

for I. A. R.

1.

Liddell, the Oxford lexicographer,
Allowed his three small daughters on this day
To row from Folly Bridge to Godstow, where
Their oarsman, Mr. Dodgson, gave them tea
Beneath a rick of hay,
Shading their minds with golden fantasy.
And it was all fool's gold,
Croquet or caucus madder than a hare,
That universe of which he sipped and told,
Mocking all grammars, codes, and theorems
Beside the spangled, blindly flowing Thames.

2.

Off to the west, in Memphis, where the sun's
Mid-morning fire beat on a wider stream,
His purpose headstrong as a river runs,
Grant closed a smoky door on aides and guards
And chewed through scheme on scheme
For toppling Vicksburg like a house of cards.
The haze at last would clear
On Hard Times Landing, Porter's wallowed guns,
The circling trenches that in just a year
Brought the starved rebels through the settling smoke
To ask for terms beside a stunted oak.

3.

The sun is not a concept but a star.
What if its rays were once conjointly blurred
By tea-fumes and a general's cigar?
Though, as for that, what grand arcanum saves
Appearances, what word
Holds all from foundering in points and waves?

No doubt the fairest game
Play only in those groves where creatures are
At one, distinct, and innocent of name,
As Alice found, who in the termless wood
Lacked words to thank the shade in which she stood.

4.

Nevertheless, no kindly swoon befell
Tree-named Linnaeus when the bald unknown
Encroached upon his memory, cell by cell,
And he, whose love of all things made had brought
Bird, beast, fish, plant, and stone
Into the reaches of his branchy thought,
Lost bitterly to mind
Their names' sweet Latin and his own as well.
Praise to all fire-fledged knowledge of the kind
That, stooped beneath a hospitable roof,
Brings only hunch and gaiety for proof,

5.

But also to Copernicus, who when
His vision leapt into the solar disc
And set the earth to wheeling, waited then
To see what slate or quadrant might exact,
Not hesitant to risk
His dream-stuff in the fitting-rooms of fact;
And honor to these States,
Which come to see that black men too are men,
Beginning, after troubled sleep, debates,
Great bloodshed, and a century's delay,
To mean what once we said upon this day.

A Shallot

The full cloves
Of your buttocks, the convex
Curve of your belly, the curved
Cleft of your sex—

Out of this corm
That's planted in strong thighs
The slender stem and radiant
Flower rise.

A Black Birch in Winter

You might not know this old tree by its bark,
Which once was striate, smooth, and glossy-dark,
So deep now are the rifts which separate
Its roughened surface into flake and plate.

Fancy might less remind you of a birch
Than of mosaic columns in a church
Like Ara Coeli or the Lateran,
Or the trenched features of an agèd man.

Still, do not be too much persuaded by
These knotty furrows and these tesserae
To think of patterns made from outside-in
Or finished wisdom in a shriveled skin.

Old trees are doomed to annual rebirth,
New wood, new life, new compass, greater girth,
And this is all their wisdom and their art—
To grow, stretch, crack, and not yet come apart.

For the Student Strikers

Go talk with those who are rumored to be unlike you,
And whom, it is said, you are so unlike.
Stand on the stoops of their houses and tell them why
You are out on strike.

It is not yet time for the rock, the bullet, the blunt
Slogan that fuddles the mind toward force.
Let the new sound in our streets be the patient sound
Of your discourse.

Doors will be shut in your faces, I do not doubt.
Yet here or there, it may be, there will start,
Much as the lights blink on in a block at evening,
Changes of heart.

They are your houses; the people are not unlike you;
Talk with them, then, and let it be done
Even for the grey wife of your nightmare sheriff
And the guardsman's son.

written for the Wesleyan *Strike News*
Spring, 1970

C Minor

Beethoven during breakfast? The human soul,
Though stalked by hollow pluckings, winning out
(While bran-flakes crackle in the cereal-bowl)
    Over despair and doubt?

You are right to switch it off and let the day
Begin at hazard, perhaps with pecker-knocks
In the sugar bush, the rancor of a jay,
    Or in the letter box

Something that makes you pause and with fixed shadow
Stand on the driveway gravel, your bent head
Scanning the snatched pages until the sad
    Or fortunate news is read.

The day's work will be disappointing or not,
Giving at least some pleasure in taking pains.
One of us, hoeing in the garden plot
    (Unless, of course, it rains)

May rejoice at the knitting of light in fennel-plumes
And dew like mercury on cabbage-hide,
Or rise and pace through too-familiar rooms,
    Balked and dissatisfied.

Shall a plate be broken? A new thing understood?
Shall we be lonely, and by love consoled?
What shall I whistle, splitting the kindling-wood?
    Shall the night-wind be cold?

How should I know? And even if we were fated
Hugely to suffer, grandly to endure,
It would not help to hear it all fore-stated
    As in an overture.

There is nothing to do with a day except to live it.
Let us have music again when the light dies
(Sullenly, or in glory) and we can give it
    Something to organize.

To His Skeleton

Why will you vex me with
These bone-spurs in the ear,
With X-rayed phlebolith
And calculus? See here,

Noblest of armatures,
The grin which bares my teeth
Is mine as yet, not yours.
Did you not stand beneath

This flesh, I could not stand,
But would revert to slime
Informous and unmanned;
And I may come in time

To wish your peace my fate,
Your sculpture my renown.
Still, I have held you straight
And mean to lay you down

Without too much disgrace
When what can perish dies.
For now then, keep your place
And do not colonize.

John Chapman

Beside the Brokenstraw or Licking Creek,
Wherever on the virginal frontier
New men with rutting wagons came to seek
Fresh paradises for the axe to clear,

John Chapman fostered in a girdled glade
Or river-flat new apples for their need,
Till half the farmsteads of the west displayed
White blossom sprung of his authentic seed.

Trusting in God, mistrusting artifice,
He would not graft or bud the stock he sold.
And what, through nature's mercy, came of this?
No sanguine crops of vegetable gold

As in Phaeacia or Hesperides,
Nor those amended fruit of harsher climes
That bowed the McIntosh or Rambo trees,
Ben Davis, Chandler, Jonathan, or Grimes,

But the old *malus malus,* double-dyed,
Eurasia's wilding since the bitter fall,
Sparse upon branches as perplexed as pride,
An apple gnarled, acidulous, and small.

Out of your grave, John Chapman, in Fort Wayne,
May you arise, and flower, and come true.
We meanwhile, being of a spotted strain
And born into a wilder land than you,

Expecting less of natural tree or man
And dubious of working out the brute,
Affix such hopeful scions as we can
To the rude, forked, and ever savage root.

April 5, 1974

The air was soft, the ground still cold.
In the dull pasture where I strolled
Was something I could not believe.
Dead grass appeared to slide and heave,
Though still too frozen-flat to stir,
And rocks to twitch, and all to blur.
What was this rippling of the land?
Was matter getting out of hand
And making free with natural law?
I stopped and blinked, and then I saw
A fact as eerie as a dream.
There was a subtle flood of steam
Moving upon the face of things.
It came from standing pools and springs
And what of snow was still around;
It came of winter's giving ground
So that the freeze was coming out,
As when a set mind, blessed by doubt,
Relaxes into mother-wit.
Flowers, I said, will come of it.

Teresa

    After the sun's eclipse,
The brighter angel and the spear which drew
A bridal outcry from her open lips,
    She could not prove it true,
Nor think at first of any means to test
By what she had been wedded or possessed.

    Not all cries were the same;
There was an island in mythology
Called by the very vowels of her name
    Where vagrants of the sea,
Changed by a wand, were made to squeal and cry
As heavy captives in a witch's sty.

    The proof came soon and plain:
Visions were true which quickened her to run
God's barefoot errands in the rocks of Spain
    Beneath its beating sun,
And lock the O of ecstasy within
The tempered consonants of discipline.

Children of Darkness

If groves are choirs and sanctuaried fanes,
What have we here?
An elm-bole cocks a bloody ear;
In the oak's shadow lies a strew of brains.
Wherever, after the deep rains,

The woodlands are morose and reek of punk,
These gobbets grow—
Tongue, lobe, hand, hoof or butchered toe
Amassing on the fallen branch half-sunk
In leaf-mold, or the riddled trunk.

Such violence done, it comes as no surprise
To notice next
How some, parodically sexed,
Puff, blush, or gape, while shameless phalloi rise,
To whose slimed heads come carrion flies.

Their gift is not for life, these creatures who
Disdain to root,
Will bear no stem or leaf, no fruit,
And, mimicking the forms which they eschew,
Make it their pleasure to undo

All that has heart and fiber. Yet of course
What these break down
Wells up refreshed in branch and crown.
May we not after all forget that Norse
Drivel of Wotan's panicked horse,

And every rumor bred of forest-fear?
Are these the brood
Of adders? Are they devil's food,

Minced witches, or the seed of rutting deer?
Nowhere does water stand so clear

As in stalked cups where pine has come to grief;
The chanterelle
And cèpe are not the fare of hell;
Where coral schools the beech and aspen leaf
To seethe like fishes of a reef,

Light strikes into a gloom in which are found
Red disc, grey mist,
Gold-auburn firfoot, amethyst,
Food for the eye whose pleasant stinks abound,
And dead men's fingers break the ground.

Gargoyles is what they are at worst, and should
They preen themselves
On being demons, ghouls, or elves,
The holy chiaroscuro of the wood
Still would embrace them. They are good.

Part Two

FRANÇOIS VILLON:
Ballade of Forgiveness

Brothers and sisters, Celestine,
Carthusian, or Carmelite,
Street-loafers, fops whose buckles shine,
Lackeys, and courtesans whose tight
Apparel gratifies the sight,
And little ladies'-men who trot
In tawny boots of dreadful height:
I beg forgiveness of the lot.

Young whores who flash their teats in sign
Of what they hawk for men's delight,
Ape-handlers, thieves and, soused with wine,
Wild bullies looking for a fight,
And Jacks and Jills whose hearts are light,
Whistling and joking, talking rot,
Street-urchins dodging left and right:
I beg forgiveness of the lot.

Excepting for those bloody swine
Who gave me, many a morn and night,
The hardest crusts on which to dine;
Henceforth I'll fear them not a mite.
I'd belch and fart in their despite,
Were I not sitting on my cot.
Well, to be peaceful and polite,
I beg forgiveness of the lot.

May hammers, huge and heavy, smite
Their ribs, and likewise cannon-shot.
May cudgels pulverize them quite.
I beg forgiveness of the lot.

JEAN DE LA FONTAINE:
The Grasshopper and the Ant

Grasshopper, having sung her song
      All summer long,
Was sadly unprovided-for
When the cold winds began to roar:
Not one least bite of grub or fly
Had she remembered to put by.
Therefore she hastened to descant
On famine, to her neighbor Ant,
Begging the loan of a few grains
Of wheat to ease her hunger-pains
Until the winter should be gone.
"You shall be paid," said she, "upon
My honor as an animal,
Both interest and principal."
The Ant was not disposed to lend;
That liberal vice was not for her.
"What did you do all summer, friend?"
She asked the would-be borrower.
"So please your worship," answered she,
"I sang and sang both night and day."
"You sang? Indeed, that pleases me.
Then dance the winter-time away."

JOACHIM DU BELLAY:
Happy the Man

Happy the man who, journeying far and wide
As Jason or Ulysses did, can then
Turn homeward, seasoned in the ways of men,
And claim his own, and there in peace abide!

When shall I see the chimney-smoke divide
The sky above my little town: ah, when
Stroll the small gardens of that house again
Which is my realm and crown, and more beside?

Better I love the plain, secluded home
My fathers built, than bold façades of Rome;
Slate pleases me as marble cannot do;

Better than Tiber's flood my quiet Loire,
Those little hills than these, and dearer far
Than great sea winds the zephyrs of Anjou.

VOLTAIRE:
To Madame du Châtelet

If you would have my heart love on,
Grant me such years as suit the lover,
And teach my twilight to recover
 (If but it could) the flush of dawn.

Time takes my elbow now, in sign
That I must bow and turn away
From gardens where the god of wine
Divides with Love his pleasant sway.

Let us from rigorous Time obtain
What timely blessings may assuage.
Whoever will not be his age
Knows nothing of his age but pain.

Leave then to sweet and giddy youth
Those ecstasies which youth can give:
Two moments only do we live;
Let there be one for sober truth.

What! Will you leave me thus forlorn,
O tenderness, illusion, folly—
Heavenly gifts whereby I've borne
Life's bitterness and melancholy?

Two deaths we suffer. To forgo
Loving, and being loved in turn,
Is deathly pain, as now I learn.
Ceasing to live is no such woe.

Thus did I mourn the loss of all
Those years when I was young and mad,

My slow heart sighing to recall
The furious beat which once it had.

Friendship, descending from above,
Came then in mercy to my aid;
She was as kind, perhaps, as Love,
But not so ardent, and more staid.

Touched by her charms, so fresh they were,
And by her radiance calm and clear,
I followed her; yet shed a tear
That I could follow none but her.

Part Three

Flippancies

The Star System

While you're a white-hot youth, emit the rays
Which, now unmarked, shall dazzle future days.
Burn for the joy of it, and waste no juice
On hopes of prompt discovery. Produce!

Then, white with years, live wisely and survive.
Thus you may be on hand when you arrive,
And, like Antares, rosily dilate,
And for a time be gaseous and great.

2.

What's Good for the Soul Is Good for Sales

If fictive music fails your lyre, confess—
Though not, of course, to any happiness.
So it be tristful, tell us what you choose:
Hangover, Nixon on the TV news,
God's death, the memory of your rocking-horse,
Entropy, housework, Buchenwald, divorce,
Those damned flamingoes in your neighbor's yard . . .
All hangs together if you take it hard.

Two Riddles from Aldhelm

I.
Once I was water, full of scaly fish,
But now am something else, by Fortune's wish.
Through fiery torment I was made to grow
As white as ashes, or as glinting snow.

II.
Ugly I am, capacious, brazen, round,
And hang between high heaven and the ground,
Seething with billows and aglow with flame.
Thus, as it were, I'm vexed upon two fronts
By both those raging elements at once.
What's my name?

Rillons, Rillettes

RILLETTES: *Hors d'oeuvre* made up of a mash of pigmeat, usually highly seasoned. Also used for making sandwiches. The *Rillettes* enjoying the greatest popularity are the *Rillettes* and *Rillons de Tours,* but there are *Rillettes* made in many other parts of France.

RILLONS: Another name for the *Rillettes,* a pigmeat *hors d'oeuvre*. The most popular *Rillons* are those of Blois.

—*A Concise Encyclopaedia of Gastronomy,* edited by André L. Simon

Rillons, Rillettes, they taste the same,
And would by any other name,
And are, if I may risk a joke,
Alike as two pigs in a poke.

The dishes are the same, and yet
While Tours provides the best *Rillettes,*
The best *Rillons* are made in Blois.
There must be some solution.
                         Ah!—

Does Blois supply, do you suppose,
The best *Rillettes de Tours,* while those
Now offered by the chefs of Tours
Are, by their ancient standards, poor?

Clever, but there remains a doubt.
It is a thing to brood about,
Like non-non-A, infinity,
Or the doctrine of the Trinity.

The Prisoner of Zenda

At the end a
"The Prisoner of Zenda,"
The King being out of danger,
Stewart Granger
(As Rudolph Rassendyll)
Must swallow a bitter pill
By renouncing his co-star,
Deborah Kerr.

It would be poor behavia
In him and in Princess Flavia
Were they to put their own
Concerns before those of the Throne.
Deborah Kerr must wed
The King instead.

Rassendyll turns to go.
Must it be so?
Why can't they have their cake
And eat it, for heaven's sake?
Please let them have it both ways,
The audience prays.
And yet it is hard to quarrel
With a plot so moral.

One redeeming factor,
However, is that the actor
Who plays the once-dissolute King
(Who has learned through suffering
Not to drink or be mean
To his future Queen),
Far from being a stranger,
Is *also* Stewart Granger.

Part Four

JOSEPH BRODSKY:
The Funeral of Bobò

1.
Bobò is dead, but don't take off your hat.
No gesture we could make will help us bear it.
Why mount a butterfly upon the spit
Of the Admiralty tower? We'd only tear it.

On every side, no matter where you glance,
Are squares of windows. As for "What happened?"—well,
Open an empty can by way of answer
And say "Just that, as near as one can tell."

Bobò is dead. Wednesday is almost over.
On streets which offer you no place to go,
Such whiteness lies. Only the night river,
With its black water, does not wear the snow.

2.
Bobò is dead; there's sadness in this line.
O window-squares, O arches' semicircles,
And such fierce frost that if one's to be slain,
Let blazing firearms do the dirty-work.

Farewell, Bobò, my beautiful and sweet.
These tear-drops dot the page like holes in cheese.
We are too weak to follow you, and yet
To take a stand exceeds our energies.

Your image, as I here and now predict,
Whether in crackling cold or waves of heat,
Shall never dwindle—quite the reverse, in fact—
In Rossi's matchless, long, and tapering street.

3.

Bobò is dead. Something I might convey
Slips from my grasp, as bath-soap sometimes does.
Today, within a dream, I seemed to lie
Upon my bed. And there, in fact, I was.

Tear off a page, but read the date aright:
It's with a zero that our woes commence.
Without her, dreams suggest the waking state,
And squares of air push through the window-vents.

Bobò is dead. One feels an impulse, with
Half-parted lips, to murmur "Why? What for?"
It's emptiness, no doubt, which follows death.
That's likelier than Hell—and worse, what's more.

4.

You were all things, Bobò. But your decease
Has changed you. You are nothing; you are not;
Or, rather, you are a clot of emptiness—
Which also, come to think of it, is a lot.

Bobò is dead. To these round eyes, the view
Of the bare horizon-line is like a knife.
But neither Kiki nor Zazà, Bobò,
Will ever take your place. Not on your life.

Now Thursday. I believe in emptiness.
There, it's like Hell, but shittier, I've heard.
And the new Dante, pregnant with his message,
Bends to the empty page and writes a word.

ANDREI VOZNESENSKY:
Phone Booth

Someone is loose in Moscow who won't stop
Ringing my 'phone.
Whoever-it-is listens, then hangs up.
Dial tone.

What do you want? A bushel of rhymes or so?
An autograph? A bone?
Hello?
Dial tone.

Someone's lucky number, for all I know,
Is the same, worse luck, as my own.
Hello!
Dial tone.

Or perhaps it's an angel calling collect
To invite me to God's throne.
Damn, I've been disconnected.
Dial tone.

Or is it my old conscience, my power of choice
To which I've grown
A stranger, and which no longer knows my voice?
Dial tone.

Are you standing there in some subway station, stiff
And hatless in the cold,
With your finger stuck in the dial as if
In a ring of gold?

And is there, outside the booth, a desperate throng
Tapping its coins on the glass, chafing its hands,

Like a line of people who have been waiting long
To be measured for wedding-bands?

I hear you breathe and blow into some remote
Mouthpiece, and as you exhale
The lapels of my coat
Flutter like pennants in a gale.

Speak up, friend! Are you deaf and dumb as a stone?
Dial tone.

The planet's communications are broken.
I'm tired of saying *hello*.
My questions might as well be unspoken.
Into the void my answers go.

Thrown together, together
With you, with you unknown.
Hello. Hello. Hello there.
Dial tone. Dial tone. Dial tone.

ANDREI VOZNESENSKY:
An Arrow in the Wall

You'd look right with a wolf from Tambov
For sidekick and friend,
As you tear my Punjabi bow
Down from the wall, and bend it.

Your hand pulls back from the shoulder
As if measuring cloth by the yard;
The arrow pants, and is eager,
Like a nipple extended and hard.

And now, with what feminine fury,
Into the wall it goes—
All the walls of the snug and secure.
There's a woman in that, God knows!

In towers of skeletal steel, —an arrow!
In pomposities one and all.
Who says it's the electronic era?
There's an arrow in the wall!

Burn, privilege and power!
There's an arrow in the wall.
Soon, in a drained and lonely hour,
Your tears will fall.

But dark now, doubly dark,
Over rich embrasures which crawl
With elaborate moldings, your stark
Arrow is in the wall!

All right, you cheeky blonde,
Checkmate me, and I'll say

"Oh, you Olympian!," thinking fondly
Of how your belly-dimples play.

"You Scythian," I shall add, "you shrew . . ."
And you'll say, "To hell with you . . ."

*   *   *   *   *

Release, O rawhide bowstring,
The stillest arrow, a dart
So incredibly hushed, one might suppose
An angel was departing.

In public, we're barely friends,
But for years it's been going on:
Beneath my high-rise window
Dark waters run.

A deep stream of love.
A bright rapids of sorrow.
A high wall of forgiveness.
And pain's clean, piercing arrow.

NIKOLAI MORSHEN:
Two Poems

1.

A star in the sky. How many words and tears,
What promises, what wishes made upon it,
How many heart-cries! For what endless years!
What dashings-off of verse and rhyme and sonnet!

Yet to the clear mind, too, it signs from heaven:
The Magi followed it with reverence;
So did the navigators . . . Einstein, even,
Could not without some fixèd stars make sense.

Ah, to select a theme that once for all
Would captivate all men without exception—
Saint, atheist, hero, coward, freeman, thrall—
And then to realize one's high conception
On the night's canvas with a dot, just one.

What artist would not own himself outdone?

2.

Nights rolled upon the river's face,
Volcanoes flared and overflowed,
And ferns which towered into space
With paleozoic flashes glowed

When, with his Slavic eye, there crept
A saurian from paludal slime—
My reptile ancestor—and stepped
On the dry land for the first time.

He did not then, of course, predict
The spate of future generation,

Of linked phenomena in strict
And inextinguishable relation,
Or me, in that concatenation,
In whose world Planck and Blok connect!

But I . . . what breed am I, what kind?
What are my past, my destiny?
How should that far one be divined
Whose modest forebear I shall be,
Whose world's pure miracle to me,
Whose deeds, the manner of whose mind?

Hundreds of years will pass, perhaps
Millions, and then he will be there,
Remembering us across that lapse,
Our strange third partner, and our heir.

And then what magic time will do!
All distances will coalesce,
And all awareness flow into
The heaven of his consciousness.

From grey mist will materialize
His predecessors, one and all,
Whatever their degree or size,
No matter how obscure or small,

And to that joyous herd, that throng
Bound from creation and before,
You too shall certainly belong,
O my reptilian ancestor.

Part Five

The Mind-Reader

The Mind-Reader

Lui parla.

for Charles and Eula

Some things are truly lost. Think of a sun-hat
Laid for the moment on a parapet
While three young women—one, perhaps, in mourning—
Talk in the crenellate shade. A slight wind plucks
And budges it; it scuffs to the edge and cartwheels
Into a giant view of some description:
Haggard escarpments, if you like, plunge down
Through mica shimmer to a moss of pines
Amidst which, here or there, a half-seen river
Lobs up a blink of light. The sun-hat falls,
With what free flirts and stoops you can imagine,
Down through that reeling vista or another,
Unseen by any, even by you or me.
It is as when a pipe-wrench, catapulted
From the jounced back of a pick-up truck, dives headlong
Into a bushy culvert; or a book
Whose reader is asleep, garbling the story,
Glides from beneath a steamer chair and yields
Its flurried pages to the printless sea.

It is one thing to escape from consciousness
As such things do, another to be pent
In the dream-cache or stony oubliette
Of someone's head.

                    They found, when I was little,
That I could tell the place of missing objects.
I stood by the bed of a girl, or the frayed knee
Of an old man whose face was lost in shadow.
When did you miss it?, people would be saying,
Where did you see it last? And then those voices,
Querying or replying, came to sound

Like cries of birds when the leaves race and whiten
And a black overcast is shelving over.
The mind is not a landscape, but if it were
There would in such case be a tilted moon
Wheeling beyond the wood through which you groped,
Its fine spokes breaking in the tangled thickets.
There would be obfuscations, paths which turned
To dried-up stream-beds, hemlocks which invited
Through shiny clearings to a groundless shade;
And yet in a sure stupor you would come
At once upon dilapidated cairns,
Abraded moss, and half-healed blazes leading
To where, around the turning of a fear,
The lost thing shone.

                      Imagine a railway platform—
The long cars come to a cloudy halt beside it,
And the fogged windows offering a view
Neither to those within nor those without.
Now, in the crowd—forgive my predilection—
Is a young woman standing amidst her luggage,
Expecting to be met by you, a stranger.
See how she turns her head, the eyes engaging
And disengaging, pausing and shying away.
It is like that with things put out of mind,
As the queer saying goes: a lost key hangs
Trammeled by threads in what you come to see
As the webbed darkness of a sewing-basket,
Flashing a little; or a photograph,
Misplaced in an old ledger, turns its bled
Oblivious profile to rebuff your vision,
Yet glistens with the fixative of thought.
What can be wiped from memory? Not the least
Meanness, obscenity, humiliation,
Terror which made you clench your eyes, or pulse
Of happiness which quickened your despair.

Nothing can be forgotten, as I am not
Permitted to forget.

                    It was not far
From that to this—this corner café table
Where, with my lank grey hair and vatic gaze,
I sit and drink at the receipt of custom.
They come here, day and night, so many people:
Sad women of the quarter, dressed in black,
As to a black confession; blinking clerks
Who half-suppose that Taurus ruminates
Upon their destinies; men of affairs
Down from Milan to clear it with the magus
Before they buy or sell some stock or other;
My fellow-drunkards; fashionable folk,
Mocking and ravenously credulous,
And skeptics bent on proving me a fraud
For fear that some small wonder, unexplained,
Should leave a fissure in the world, and all
Saint Michael's host come flapping back.

                              I give them
Paper and pencil, turn away and light
A cigarette, as you have seen me do;
They write their questions; fold them up; I lay
My hand on theirs and go into my frenzy,
Raising my eyes to heaven, snorting smoke,
Lolling my head as in the fumes of Delphi,
And then, with shaken, spirit-guided fingers,
Set down the oracle. All that, of course,
Is trumpery, since nine times out of ten
What words float up within another's thought
Surface as soon in mine, unfolding there
Like paper flowers in a water-glass.
In the tenth case, I sometimes cheat a little.

That shocks you? But consider: what I do
Cannot, so most conceive, be done at all,
And when I fail, I am a charlatan
Even to such as I have once astounded—
Whereas a tailor can mis-cut my coat
And be a tailor still. I tell you this
Because you know that I have the gift, the burden.
Whether or not I put my mind to it,
The world usurps me ceaselessly; my sixth
And never-resting sense is a cheap room
Black with the anger of insomnia,
Whose wall-boards vibrate with the mutters, plaints,
And flushings of the race.

                          What should I tell them?
I have no answers. *Set your fears at rest,*
I scribble when I must. *Your paramour*
Is faithful, and your spouse is unsuspecting.
You were not seen, that day, beneath the fig-tree.
Still, be more cautious. When the time is ripe,
Expect promotion. I foresee a message
From a far person who is rich and dying.
You are admired in secret. If, in your judgment,
Profit is in it, you should take the gamble.
As for these fits of weeping, they will pass.

It makes no difference that my lies are bald
And my evasions casual. It contents them
Not to have spoken, yet to have been heard.
What more do they deserve, if I could give it,
Mute breathers as they are of selfish hopes
And small anxieties? Faith, justice, valor,
All those reputed rarities of soul
Confirmed in marble by our public statues—
You may be sure that they are rare indeed

Where the soul mopes in private, and I listen.
Sometimes I wonder if the blame is mine,
If through a sullen fault of the mind's ear
I miss a resonance in all their fretting.
Is there some huge attention, do you think,
Which suffers us and is inviolate,
To which all hearts are open, which remarks
The sparrow's weighty fall, and overhears
In the worst rancor a deflected sweetness?
I should be glad to know it.

                         Meanwhile, saved
By the shrewd habit of concupiscence,
Which, like a visor, narrows my regard,
And drinking studiously until my thought
Is a blind lowered almost to the sill,
I hanker for that place beyond the sparrow
Where the wrench beds in mud, the sun-hat hangs
In densest branches, and the book is drowned.
Ah, you have read my mind. One more, perhaps . . .
A mezzo-litro. Grazie, professore.

Notes

The Eye: St. Lucy (S. Lucia), patroness of eyesight, perceived Dante's plight in Canto II of the *Inferno.*

In Limbo: Plato recounts the vision of Er at the close of his *Republic.*

Peter: John's gospel says that it was Peter who "smote the high priest's servant." Mark, Luke and John all tell how Peter "sat with the servants, and warmed himself at the fire."

Cottage Street: Edna Ward was Mrs. Herbert D. Ward, my wife's mother. The poet Sylvia Plath (1932–1963) was the daughter of one of Mrs. Ward's Wellesley friends. The recollection is probably composite, but it is true in essentials.

The Fourth of July: Lewis Carroll first told of Alice's adventures on July 4, 1862. Vicksburg capitulated to General Grant on July 4, 1863. Of the "stunted oak," the General wrote in his *Memoirs,*

> At three o'clock Pemberton appeared at the point suggested in my verbal message, accompanied by the same officers who had borne his letter of the morning. Generals Ord, McPherson, Logan, and A. J. Smith, and several officers of my staff, accompanied me. Our place of meeting was on a hillside within a few hundred feet of the rebel lines. Near by stood a stunted oak-tree, which was made historical by the event. It was but a short time before the last vestige of its body, root and limb had disappeared, the fragments taken as trophies. Since then the same tree has furnished as many cords of wood, in the shape of trophies, as "The True Cross."

The "termless wood" may be found in *Through the Looking Glass,* Chapter III. In *The Life of Sir Charles Linnaeus* (London, 1794), D. H. Stoever wrote:

> Several of his relatives, who had quitted the Plough for the Muses, in the last century, changed their family name with their profession, and borrowed the names of LINDELIUS,

or TILIANDER (Linden-*tree-man*), of a lofty Linden-tree, which still stood in our time, in the vicinity of their native place, between *Tomsboda* and *Linnhult;* a custom not unfrequent in *Sweden,* to take fresh appellations from natural objects. The father of LINNAEUS, as the first learned man of his family, could not withstand following the example which his kindred had set before him.

Owing to a stroke, Linnaeus lost in his latter years "the knowledge even of his own name." (Loren Eiseley, *Darwin's Century.*)

For the Student Strikers: This was written one afternoon at the request of Wesleyan students, during a "strike" against U.S. military actions in Southeast Asia. The poem supports a student-proposed "canvassing" program, under which the students were to go from door to door in the city of Middletown, discussing their views with the citizens. As the poem did not flatter the students in the manner to which they were accustomed, it was at first thrown into the wastebasket at the offices of *Strike News,* but later retrieved and published.

To His Skeleton: A phlebolith is a vein-stone.

John Chapman was also known as "John Appleseed." With few exceptions, apple trees raised from the seed of cultivated varieties do not "come true," but revert to the wild Eurasian type.

Teresa: The name of Circe's island was Aeaea.

Children of Darkness: Fungi do not have true roots, stems, leaves, or fruit, and do not increase by means of chlorophyll and light. They were early associated with darkness, snake-pits, witches, devils, and evil in general. The Fly Agaric was said, in folklore, to grow from the bloody slaver of Wotan's horse, pursued by devils. Among the plants mentioned here are Ear, Coral, Disc and Mist Fungi; Morels; Earth Tongues; Rusty Hooves; Stinkhorns (*Phallus impudicus*); Stalked Saucers, and Dead Man's Fingers (*Xylaria polymorpha*).

66

François Villon: Ballade of Forgiveness: Villon spent the summer of 1461 in prison at Meung-sur-Loire. The third stanza refers to his jailers, and "the hardest crusts" may imply torture.

Two Riddles from Aldhelm: The answers are Salt and Cauldron. Aldhelm, Bishop of Sherborne, died in 709; he was the author of 100 Latin riddles.

Joseph Brodsky: The Funeral of Bobò: The poem concerns a young woman who was drowned, under mysterious circumstances, in the Gulf of Finland.

For linguistic aid in translating from the Russian, I owe thanks to Professors Simon Karlinsky and Carl R. Proffer.